Based on Song of Songs

Loving Jesus

Bride and Groom

Chelsea Kong

Printed in 2023, Made in Toronto, Canada
ISBN: 978-1-990399-39-8
Library and Archives Canada

A woman loves a man and tells him.
The man and woman talk about their looks.
This is how love starts.

The woman says, "She is rose in the Plain of Sharon."
The man says, "She is a Lilly in the Valley. "
We are special in Jesus' eyes, too.

We need to be ready to love.
Our mind, body, and feelings can trick us.
We can make mistakes and need to learn.

Young love makes a woman and man glad.
They imagine and explore just like our love for Jesus.
We need to be careful of those who dislike us.

Jesus loves us more than wine.
You are special in His eyes.
His banner over us is love.

There are times we wait a long time.
God works even when we see nothing.
He will hide us and also hide from us.

love

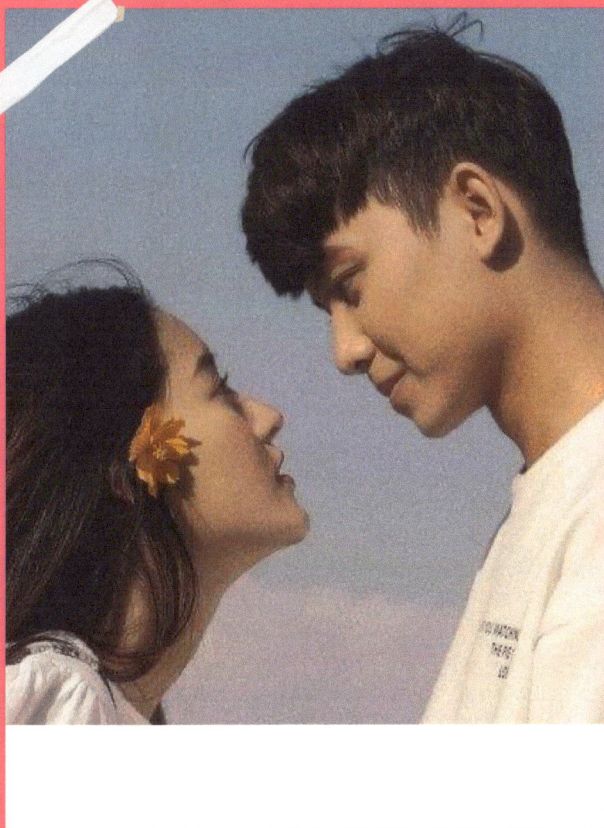

Love makes us worry about the other person.
Ask God, Jesus, and the Holy Spirit to teach us.
He shows us things and uses people to talk to us.

When love grows, we find it hard.
Our love is tested, and the enemy makes fun of us.
We miss our lover, and it hurts our heart.

The devil treats us badly.
The devil uses people to hurt us.
He makes us sad, gives us pain, and is lonely.

We need to remember God and Jesus' love for us. Life will not be easy, and we need to let go of things. We may wait a long time for God to help us.

We will tell others we belong to Jesus.
We do not always understand things.
People may look down on us and hurt us more.

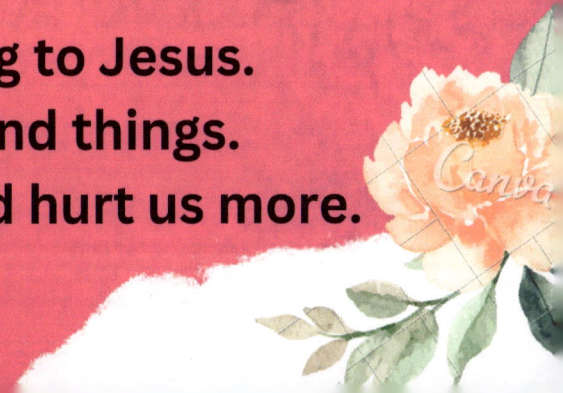

We need to fully trust God.
Everything will work out for our good.
Be strong and hold on to what Jesus told us.

God loves us and nothing can change that.
He will give you good words to help you.
His angels are always with us.

Read the Bible, worship, and thank Him every day.
Pray, stay alone with Him, and obey Him.
Ask God to forgive you when you make a mistake.

People may feel God when we pray.
Holy Spirit will give us power and gifts to help others.
It may take time for us to change and be new.

Holy Spirit will give us His words to speak.
We will love God, Jesus, and the Holy Spirit more.
Our heart will hold more and give more.

Keep your eyes on Jesus all the time.
Watch and pray to keep the devil away.
We look for God, and He is not there.

We may have times God doesn't come to us.
The devil will tell us lies and God may be silent.
Sometimes we feel God is playing a game.

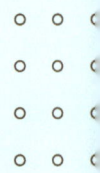

We grow in our love and grow in God through trust.
We let God change our heart and people see it.
We want him to fill our hearts and to work with us.

Jesus makes us new and we become more like Him.
He gets jealous when we love people or things more.
We become excited when He meets us.

Jesus wants us to follow closely and quickly.
We will dream about Him.
He tells secrets things in our dreams.

Pray for Jesus' blood to cover you.
He keeps you from the devil's attack.
Fast and pray as God leads you.

The devil fights harder to make us fall.
He wants to see us go far away from God.
He sets traps with good things we like.

LOVE

We must fight to stay in love with Jesus.
Use God's Word as our sword to fight back.
It can make us tired when God is not there.

Pray by the Holy Spirit and with His Words.
God will make us strong against the devil.
The angels and Holy Spirit help us.

Do not give up!
God's Word gives us victory over the devil.
Keep praying, reading the Bible, worshipping God.

Know who you are in Jesus.
The devil will leave us alone.
Jesus heals and makes us new again.

We become more like Jesus and love Jesus more.
We are not afraid of the devil and he cannot stop us.
Tell him to go from your life and never return.

We may not see any change.
Jesus wants us to keep strong in our faith.
People will see the change in you.

Jesus shows us how much He loves us.
He reminds us of His promises.
This is the love of man and woman being one.

God keeps working inside our heart.
We feel some pain sometimes.
We love what Jesus loves and hate what He hates.

We need to forgive others and love them.
We need to grow the fruit of the Holy Spirit.
The Lord is our protection.

He waits for us to be ready for more.
We will have more tests, but we will win.
We live by the Holy Spirit and walk by faith.

When we win, we grow in our love for God and Jesus.
We want to be with Him more and more.
Become wise as the virgins and be ready for Jesus.

Our love for Jesus becomes so strong.
It grows deeper and is more than feelings.
Show the love of Jesus in all you do.

We will share everything with Jesus.
He will answer us and share His heart.
We will love people the way He does.

Jesus will make you more beautiful.
He has a place for us in heaven.
We need to know Jesus well.

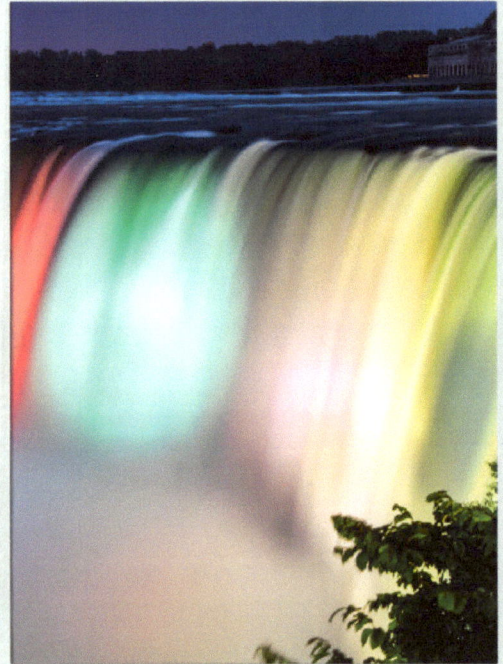

Do you love Jesus more than the world?
Will you give Him everything?
Do you see only Jesus and want to be with Him?

Are you ready for Jesus?
Did you do what Jesus told you to do?
Do you love others like Jesus does?

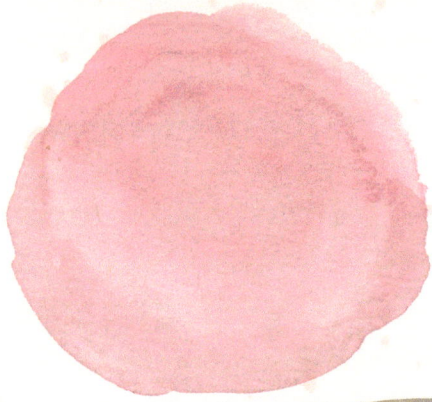

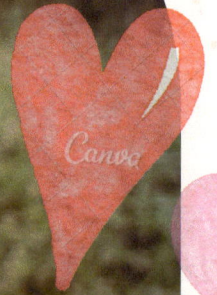

We lose the love for the things in the world.
We only want Jesus and become more like Him.
We will want to help others.

God wants us for Himself.
We must take care of what God gives us.
Hold on to God's word.

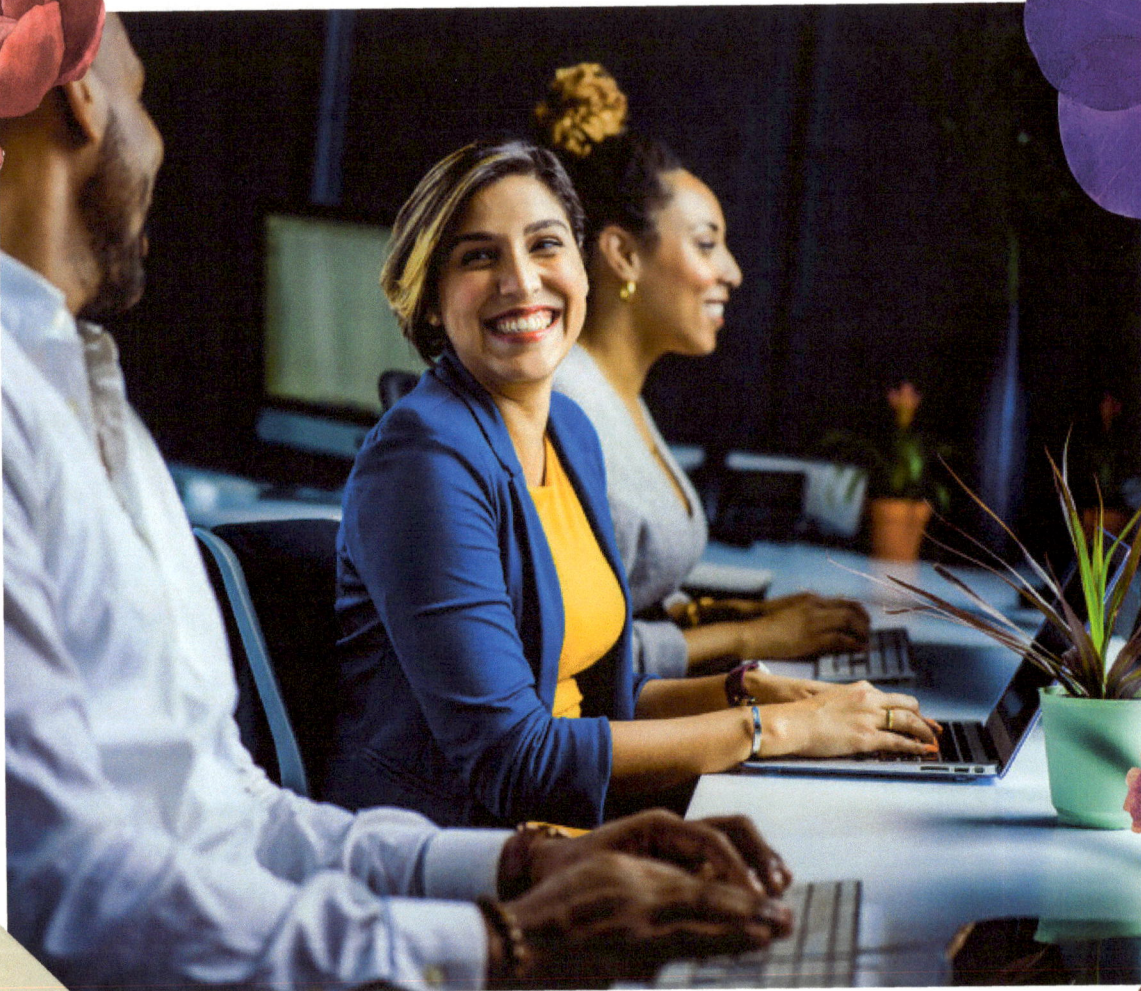

People feel God is with us when we are around them.
People may also want Jesus.
We need to share Jesus with others.

Pray with others and for others.
Others don't want Jesus will go away or get angry.
Jesus will touch people through you.

God will never leave us.
He will love us as His Bride.
People will know that we belong to Him.

Love

Jesus will come for us and take us to heaven.
We are the bride, and He is our groom.
Jesus takes us to His wedding feast.

We have a new home in a new heaven and new earth.
We will have a new body and new clothing to wear.
We will be with Jesus forever.

SALVATION PRAYER

God, I know I sinned against you. Forgive me for the wrong that I have done. I believe that Jesus Christ died on the cross for me. That He rose from the grave so that after three days. I can have His long-lasting life. Come into my heart to be my Lord and Savior. I choose to turn away from my sins and I choose to follow you. Lead me to walk with you. Keep me safe and teach me your ways. Stop every bad thing in my life that has an open door to hurt me. Close those doors. Holy Spirit, fill me now in Jesus' name. Amen.

BAPTISM IN THE HOLY SPIRIT

Jesus, you are the one that fills me with Your Spirit. Come, Holy Spirit, and come into my life and fill me to overflow with Your presence. Come with your fire too. Thank you for the gift of tongues in Jesus' name. Amen.

Open your mouth and let the words come out that God gives you. It will be words you don't know what they mean. You can ask God what it means. You need to let Him talk through you every day to grow this gift.

He will bring you closer to God and you will know Jesus more. You will have power from God to do great things and know things.

PRAYER

Jesus, I want to love you more than anything in this world. Change my heart to become like you more and more every day. Thank you for the Holy Spirit and your angels to help me. Guard my heart from all evil. Keep me in your ways. Make me ready for you when you come back for your bride, in Jesus' name. Amen.

Message from the Author

Our love for God, Jesus, and Holy Spirit becomes rich. The devil can't stop us and when he tries to fight he loses. He leaves us alone and looks for us to use against us. We must keep growing strong in the Lord. Jesus told us that the devil can't win against us. He has given us God's armour to protect us and the Holy Spirit to teach and guide us.

REFERENCES

Biblegateway. International Children's Bible (ICB)
https://www.biblegateway.com/

OTHER PRODUCTS

Knowing God

How to Hear God's Voice

New Life in Jesus

Loving Israel

God's Gifts

Meeting God

Word Power

Fruit of the Spirit

The Tabernacle

Bride for Jesus

A Life of Prayer

Live Free

Who am I in Jesus

Walk in Love

God's Favor

Man of God

Woman of God

How to Use Money

God's Wisdom

Fasting

See Jerusalem and Bethany

First Fruit Offering

Feast of Trumpets

Day of Atonement

Feast of Tabernacles

Counting the Omer

Festival of Lights

Glory, Presence, and Holy Spirit

Live in God's Presence

Pentecost

See Galilee, Nazareth, and Tiberias

Hear God Speak

Knowing Jesus

Knowing Holy Spirit

A Healthy Life and Healthy Life Work Book

Smokey the Cat

Passover Unleavened Bread

Resurrection Life

The Blessing

Chelsea's Psalms and Poems

Revival

Chelsea Learns Hebrew

Thanksgiving

Give Thanks

Jesus Birth

Proverbs 31 Woman

OTHER PRODUCTS

Coming soon

Colours in the BIble

Your Daily Meal: Chelsea's Photo Album

ABC's of Faith

Devotionals

31 Day Devotional

Puzzle Books

Biblical Puzzle Book Vol 1-5

Bible Puzzles for Young Children Book 1-3

Biblical Puzzle for Children Books 1-5

Teaching Series

How to Hear God's Voice Teaching Guide & Audio Book

Relationship with God, Jesus, Holy Spirit Guide

Knowing God, Jesus, Holy Spirit Guide & Audio Book

Flowing in the Prophetic

Teaching (Non-Sale on my website)

Purim

Passover

Resurrection

More books to come!

BOOK REVIEWS

More books on Amazon, Kobo, and Barnes and Noble, and Smashwords.
https://chelseak532002550.wordpress.com/

More books on Amazon, Kobo, and Barnes and Noble, and Smashwords.
https://www.amazon.com/author/chelseakong

Please leave a review and share with friends to help the author continue to write more books to reach more readers. Thank you so much for your support.

Review!

About
CHELSEA KONG

She is a writer, creative arts and digital media artist, skilled administration professional, and podcaster. Chelsea also served in a variety of roles, from audiovisual, photography, to assisting on the worship team, and ministry team. She also has a passion for families being united.

Chelsea has been a guest on Unity Live Radio, The Lady Tracey Show, and How to Live for Christ and is highly recommended by a Proud Christian blog. She is also a guest blogger. A few of her books have been featured in YourAuthorHub, etc. She graduated from Hotel and Restaurant Management, Digital Media Arts, Office Administration, Payroll Professional, and experience working with children. Chelsea lives in Toronto, Canada. She mainly writes children's books, stories, bridal writing, poems, lyrics for songs, words of encouragement, blessings, prayers, and jokes. The author of How to Hear the Voice of God, the Bridal Collection, Knowing God, etc. She also has her own Bible Puzzle books and other inspired products. Her podcast channel is called Chelsea K on Anchor, Spotify, and iTunes.

Please check my website to find out more:
https://chelseak532002550.wordpress.com/

www.ingramcontent.com/pod-product-compliance
Lightning Source LLC
Chambersburg PA
CBHW042013080426
42734CB00003B/67